Religious Studies Ethics Year 1

OCR Revision Guide (New Spec)

Completely Revised

Peter Baron

Published by Active Education

www.peped.org

This edition 2016

ISBN-13: 978-1541086029
ISBN-10: 1541086023

Handouts, powerpoints, extracts, articles, links, reviews, news and revision materials available on www.peped.org

The peped.org website allows students and teachers to explore Philosophy of Religion and Ethics through handouts, film clips, presentations, case studies, extracts, games and academic articles.

Pitched just right, and so much more than a text book, here is a place to engage with critical reflection whatever your level. Marked student essays are also posted.

We also sell digital resources including Teaching Packs for the 2009 and 2016 specifications (full lesson plans, powerpoints, starter activities, and extracts for the entire course), marked essay packs, and a booklet giving full guidelines on how to answer questions on our summer exam paper predictions.

Contents

The Examination

The OCR Year 1 Ethics Course narrows the applied topics down to two - euthanasia and business ethics, whilst retaining emphasis on the key moral theories of Utilitarianism, Situation Ethics, Kantian ethics and Natural Law. We are required to apply Natural Law and Situation Ethics to issues surrounding euthanasia, and Kant and Utilitarianism to business ethics.

• **CASE STUDIES** are an excellent way of thinking through issues surrounding applied ethics - such as Diane Pretty in 2002 (euthanasia) or Enron in 2003 (business ethics). You will find these on the website www.peped.org

• **MAPPING THE THEORIES** gives a sequence of thought which goes from a starting point (such as **SYNDERESIS** for Natural Law) to a finishing point (**EUDAIMONIA** for Natural Law) and then links the concepts together to form an analysis.

• **TEXTBOOKS** may have their place, but you are examined on the syllabus alone, so study it carefully. There are many ways of doing and thinking about ethics. Wilcockson and Wilkinson (2016) frequently take a Roman Catholic perspective (eg quotes from encyclicals and the Catholic Catechism). But you could just as well quote from the Church of England, the United Reformed Church or the Baptist or Orthodox churches to gain a Christian perspective. Or line up a humanist or atheist perspective against it. Textbooks also include extra material which is not strictly necessary to be an A grade candidate.

Introduction to Ethics

Key Terms

- **NORMATIVE ETHICS** - how norms (values of good and bad) are derived and then applied to the real world.

- **META-ETHICS** - the meaning and function of ethical language.

- **OBJECTIVE TRUTH -** the view that truth is testable by observation and experience.

- **RELATIVISM** - the view that all values (norms) are simply expressions of culture and there are no universal, unchanging values of 'good'.

- **SUBJECTIVE TRUTH** - the view that truth is something that depends on an individual perception or belief system and cannot be shared objectively.

- **SITUATION ETHICS** - a theory of ethics that holds that what is good or bad needs to be assessed according to what maximises love in any situation.

- **TELEOLOGICAL ETHICS** - ethics that focuses on the end or telos of an action, for example, Situation Ethics focuses on love as the highest end or purpose.

- **DEONTOLOGICAL** - ethics that focuses on the duty (deon) or rule.

Normative Ethics

Asks the question "how should I act, morally speaking?" or "what ought I to do?"

A norm is a "value" i.e. something I think of as good. The normative theories we study at AS or Year 1 (OCR) are: Natural Law, Kantian ethics, Utilitarianism and Situation Ethics. Each theory derives the idea of goodness a different way: Natural Law with reference to the true rational purpose of human beings; Utilitarianism, with reference to the one assumed norm of happiness and its maximisation; Kantian ethics, by an a priori method of taking an imaginative step backwards and universalising our action; and Situation Ethics by maximising the one norm of love in a given situation.

Meta-Ethics

Meta-ethics studies the foundations of ethics and meaning of ethical terms (what does it mean to say something is good?). It particularly focuses on ethical language. Meta-ethics is studied at **A2** level. Key meta-ethical questions include:

- "Is morality absolute – applying everywhere and for all time, or is it relative, specific to a time and place – a culture, situation or viewpoint?"

- "Is there such a thing as a moral fact?"

- "What do different ethical theorists mean by 'good'?"

- "Is goodness a natural feature of the world to be accessed and measured (a bit like science)?"

Applied Ethics

Applies ethical theories to real world situations. The applied issues at AS or Year 1 (OCR) are:

- **Euthanasia applied to Natural Law and Situation Ethics**

- **Business Ethics applied to Utilitarianism and Kantian ethics.**

A key question in applied ethics is: how do I apply the norm derived by any one ethical theory to the issues surrounding euthanasia and business ethics? The syllabus helps us identify these issues: sanctity of human life, quality of life and autonomy for euthanasia, and globalisation, whistle-blowing, and the interests of stakeholders for business ethics. We could also add our own, such as slippery slope arguments in euthanasia and environmental responsibility for business.

Moreover, we can ask the question generally: is there any difference between an **ACT** (doing something deliberately) and an **OMISSION** (failing to do something)? For example, in cases of euthanasia is failing to offer life support the same ethically as deliberately administering a drug that will kill?

Deontological

Acts are right or wrong in themselves (intrinsically) – it is not about consequences. Often stresses the rules or duty (Kantian ethics is pure deontology and Natural Law has both teleological and deontological aspects). **DEON** is Greek for duty.

Teleological

Teleological theories (**TELOS** = end in Greek) focuses on the purpose and consequences of actions. An action is good only if it brings about beneficial consequences and so fulfils the good purpose (it is instrumentally good, not intrinsically because actions are means to some other end like happiness or pleasure), for example, Utilitarianism (good purpose is maximising happiness) and Situation Ethics (good purpose is max mising agape love). Joseph Fletcher declares: "the end justifies the means, nothing else".

Four Questions To Ask Of Ethical Theories

- **Derivation**: How does the moral theory derive (produce) the idea of goodness?

- **Application**: How can we apply the "good" to choices we make, such as Natural Law to euthanasia or Kantian ethics to business?

- **Realism**: How realistic is the theory with reference to human psychology and our own experience?

- **Motivation**: Why should I be moral? How does this eth cal theory suggest I should be motivated to save a stranger in need? What stops me living my life as an ethical egoist, just putting my self-interest first?

These questions will be answered for all moral theories in the final chapter.

Key Quotes - Norms

1. "There are no absolute universal moral standards binding on all men at all times". John Ladd

2. "All men are created equal..they are endowed with certain unalienable rights". US Declaration of Independence

3. "Values are merely culturally approved habits". Ruth Benedict

4. "In its nature, the moral judgement is wholly independent of religion". William Temple

5. "The end justifies the means, nothing else". Joseph Fletcher

6. "There is no objective truth". J.L.Mackie

7. "We are in danger of falling into a tyranny of relativism". Pope Benedict

8. "The only good thing is the good will". Immanuel Kant

9. "There could still be a set of general moral norms applicable to all cultures and even recognised in most, which a culture could disregard at its own expense". Louis Pojman

10. "The Gentiles have the law written on their hearts, to which their conscience bears witness". Romans 2:14

Natural Law

A normative **DEONTOLOGICAL** theory coming from a **TELEOLOGICAL** worldview, as Aristotle argues that the good is defined by the **RATIONAL ENDS** or **FINAL CAUSES** which people by nature pursue.

"Natural Law is the sharing in the eternal law by intelligent creatures" argues **AQUINAS** and calls these rational ends **OBJECTS OF THE WILL**. Key assumptions are that we have a fixed human nature, there is an eternal law in God himself, and the **SYNDERESIS** principle – that all human beings naturally share a conscience that guides us to "do good and avoid evil". Aquinas calls synderesis "the first principle of the natural law" and it is one of two words he uses for conscience.

Key Terms

- **NATURAL LAW** - "right reason in agreement with nature", (Cicero). "The sharing in the eternal law by rational creatures', (Aquinas).

- **SYNDERESIS** - the first principle that we by nature seek to do good and avoid evil – or have an innate knowledge of first principles (the primary precepts). This makes the theory universal in application (it applies to a Christian believer and a non-believer or believer of another religion).

- **PRIMARY PRECEPTS** - principles known innately which define the rational ends or goods of human existence and define the good goals we pursue - these are general and do not change.

- **SECONDARY PRECEPTS** - applications of the primary precepts using human reason, which are not absolute and so may change. For example, Pope Francis has given hints that the Catholic church may revise its absolute ban on contraception as a violation of the primary precept of reproduction.

- **APPARENT GOODS** - acts done from reason which do not correspond to the natural law.

- **REAL GOODS** - acts done from human reason which correspond to the natural law.

- **NATURAL RIGHTS** - rights given to human beings because of their very nature as human. These are enshrined in the US Declaration of Independence which starts: 'we hold these rights to be inalienable'.

- **ETERNAL LAW** - the law as conceived by God and existing as an ideal of all law and projected in the design of the Universe.

- **DIVINE LAW** - the law revealed to humankind in the Bible, such as the ten commandments in the book of Exodus or the beatitudes in Matthew.

- **HUMAN LAW** - the laws we establish by human reason as our social laws.

Synderesis: 'each precious child, born with the desire to do good, and avoid evil'

Aquinas' Argument

AQUINAS sought to reconcile Christian thought with Greek thinking (**ARISTOTLE**'s works) discovered in Islamic libraries at the **FALL OF TOLEDO** (1085), when Christian armies reconquered Spain.

He sees goodness in the **DIVINE ESSENCE** (nature of God) which has a purpose – the **ETERNAL LAW** – reflected in our **HUMAN NATURE** and the ends we rationally pursue. A key assumption Aquinas makes is called the **SYNDERESIS** principle that we naturally "do good and avoid evil" – which is the opposite of the **REFORMATION** assumption that "all have sinned and fall short of God's glory" (Romans 3:23).

We are born with good natures, able to reason and so pursue good ends or objects of the will. The **DIVINE LAW** reflects God's eternal law and is revealed in holy Scripture (eg Ten Commandments of Exodus 20). From these observable God-designed rational ends (goals) we get the **PRIMARY PRECEPTS**.

Primary Precepts

There are five observable "goods" or rational ends we pursue. (Acronym **POWER**).

- **P**reservation of life

- **O**rdered society

- **W**orship of God

- **E**ducation and

- **R**eproduction

These reflect the **DIVINE WILL** because God designed us with a rational nature in His image. Notice that **VERITATIS SPLENDOR** (1995 Papal document) has subtlely changed these – Worship of God becomes **APPRECIATION OF BEAUTY** (to fit with our agnostic age), and it adds concern for the environment to reflect the new emphasis on stewardship rather than **DOMINION** (Genesis 1:24 "and let man have dominion over the earth"). Note that the commitment to environmental value is weak in Veritatis Splendor: "to preserve and cultivate the riches of the natural world'. These subtle changes may indicate that Natural Law is not as **ABSOLUTE** as we sometimes think. The fourth type of law is **HUMAN LAW**.

For society to flourish (Greek telos (purpose) of **EUDAIMONIA** sees happiness as personal and social flourishing) we need to bring our human law in line with the **ETERNAL LAW** of God, or put another way, make it appropriate for rational human beings to fulfil their Godly destiny – being with God forever, and being Christlike.

The Four Laws

Natural Law can be mapped in two ways. The first way is **TELEOLOGICAL** because it focuses on the end or telos of human behaviour - to achieve a flourishing or fulfilled life, **EUDAIMONIA** (see mindmap). Aristotle begins Nichomachean Ethcis by arguing 'the intrinsic good is that at which all things aim' - a broad and general goal.

The second way is by focusing on duties created by the four laws.

- **ETERNAL LAW** - a blueprint in the mind of God of the principles by which God made and controls the universe, which we discover by observation **A POSTERIORI** - through scientific experiments for example, or **A PRIORI** by pure reason as in Mathematics.

- **NATURAL LAW** - the moral law inherent in human beings, discoverable by reason, and expressed in the rational goals which humans by nature pursue.

- **DIVINE LAW** - expressed in the Bible (eg the Ten Commandments or Sermon on the Mount) and then interpreted and applied by human reason.

- **HUMAN LAW** - formulated as codes that create the common good and the precept of an ordered society, and should reflect the eternal law in order to be seen to be good and just. If a ruler ordered that we kill all female babies this would be bad for human flourishing and contrary to the **PRMARY PRECEPT** of preservation of life. and so an unjust and 'bad' law.

These can be represented as a diamond with eternal law at the top. Note that we 'are only required to obey secular rulers to the extent that justice requires' (Aquinas). Evil laws should be resisted and disobeyed.

Secondary Precepts

These are **APPLICATIONS** of the **PRIMARY PRECEPTS** and may change eg as our society changes, science advances our understanding of the Divine Mind, or a situation demands it (eg Thou shalt not kill gets suspended in times of war).

Aquinas suggests **POLYGAMY** (many wives) may sometimes be justified. We don't necessarily have to accept Roman Catholic applications eg Abortion is tantamount to murder, Euthanasia breaks the **SANCTITY OF LIFE**, contraception goes against the primary natural purpose of sex, which is **REPRODUCTION**, and homosexual behaviour is described as **INTRINSICALLY DISORDERED** (the phrase used in **HUMANAE VITAE**, 1968).

There is another assumption here, that there is one human nature – heterosexual- and so there can't be a gay nature. Modern Psychology (eg Carl **JUNG**) suggests we have male and female aspects to our natures and Chinese philosophy has always talked in terms of **YING** and **YANG** – the two aspects of our nature.

Phronesis

Practical wisdom (phronesis in Greek) is important because we need to cultivate right judgment to identify the non-absolute **SECONDARY PRECEPTS**. "Practical wisdom requires the application to action, which is the goal of practical reason" (Aquinas). So Natural Law has a situational aspect - we need to assess and 'the more specific the conditions are, the greater the probability of an exception arising', argues Aquinas (ST I -II q.94 a.4c). **SYNDERESIS** gives us a general orientation towards the good but **PHRONESIS** fills in the details of how to apply any primary precept.

Apparent Goods

We cannot consciously sin because our nature is such that we believe we are "doing good and avoiding evil" – the **SYNDERESIS** principle – even when practising genocide. However, though we rationalise it, this clearly breaks the **ETERNAL LAW** reflected in the **NATURAL LAW** that most rational humans want to **PRESERVE LIFE** (primary precept **P** of **POWER** acronym above). We cannot flourish if we break the Natural Law – in this sense we are being sub-human and irrational (even though we believe otherwise). **AQUINAS** calls these **APPARENT GOODS** – which we mistakenly believe (eg Hitler's genocide) are **REAL GOODS**. We can sin, but not consciously, which is why Evangelical Christians dislike Natural Law theory – arguing it is unrealistic (our very reason is distorted by sin) and unbiblical (it seems to deny Paul's teaching on **ORIGINAL SIN**, inherited from Adam after the **FALL** in Genesis 3).

Two Goods In Conflict

In business ethics the principles of truthfulness and loyalty to the company come into conflict when a whistleblower discovers evidence of wrongdoing, or with euthanasia, when doctors increase the morphine dose to alleviate pain in the knowledge that they will kill the patient. **DOUBLE EFFECT** argues that if the primary effect results from a good intention (alleviate suffering) then the secondary effect isn't evil (causing a death). Notice you can only make the judgement by considering **CONSEQUENCES** and the end of patient welfare. Aquinas argues: "moral actions take their character from what is intended" and so if I act in self defence and unintentionally kill someone I am not doing wrong as long as the action is **PROPORTIONATE.**

Strengths

AUTONOMOUS AND RATIONAL: Natural law is an autonomous, rational theory and it is wrong to say that you have to believe in God to make sense of it. Aquinas speaks of "the pattern of life lived according to reason". You could be a Darwinian atheist and believe in natural law derived by empirical observation, with the primary precept of survival (Aquinas' preservation of life). Richard **DAWKINS** (The Selfish Gene) goes so far as to argue for a natural genetic tendency to be altruistic: a lust to be nice. "The theory of Natural Law suggests..morality is **AUTONOMOUS**. It has its own questions, its own methods of answering them, and its own standards of truth, and religious considerations are not the point". Rachels (2006:56)

AN EXALTED VIEW OF HUMAN BEINGS: We use reason to work out how to live. So we are not slaves to our passions or our genes. Natural

Law has a purpose: a flourishing society and a person fulfilled and happy - **EUDAIMONIA**. It is not ultimately about restricting us by rules, but setting us free to fulfil our proper purpose or **TELOS**, inherent in our design: to rationally assent to personal growth. If we can agree on our purpose we can agree on what morality is for. Moreover, we don't have to accept the fact/value division inherent in Moore or Ayer's philosophy. "The natural world is not to be regarded merely as a realm of facts, devoid of value or purpose. Instead, the world is conceived to be a **RATIONAL ORDER** with value and purpose built into its very nature". Rachels (2006: 50)

FLEXIBLE: Natural Law is not inflexible. The primary precepts may be general and unchanging, but as Aquinas argued, **SECONDARY PRECEPTS** can change depending on circumstances, culture and worldview. Aquinas calls them 'proximate conclusions of reason'. The Doctrine of **DOUBLE EFFECT** is also a way to escape the moral dilemmas which exist when two rules conflict, (See Louis Pojman 2006: 47-51) – so not as **ABSOLUTE** as textbooks suggest.

Weaknesses

A FIXED HUMAN NATURE: Aquinas believes in one fixed, shared human nature with certain natural properties eg heterosexual. But evidence suggests there are gay genes and so there is no one natural human nature, but many. This is actually a form of the **NATURALISTIC FALLACY**, the movement from an "is" to an "ought". "It may be that sex does produce babies, but it does not follow that sex ought or ought not to be engaged in only for that purpose. Facts are one thing, values are another". Rachels (2006:52)

AN OPTIMISTIC VIEW: Aquinas believes that we **INNATELY** (we are bom with) have a "tendency to do good and avoid evil", **SYNDERESIS**. This is in contrast with Augustine who believes that, due to the Fall, we are born into sin, the sin of Adam, or perhaps the view of psychologists like Freud, that natural selfishness becomes moralised by upbringing and socialisation.

IMMORAL OUTCOMES: Natural Law has been interpreted to ban contraception, because this interferes with the natural primary precept of reproduction. But a. it's not clear that sex is exclusively for reproduction, in fact, the function of bonding may be primary and b. the consequence of this policy in Africa has had evil effects of the spread of **AIDS** and the birth of **AIDS** infected children who often become orphans living on the streets.

Possible Exam Questions

1. "Natural Law does not present a helpful method for making moral decisions". Discuss

2. "Moral decisions should be based on duty, not purpose". Assess with reference to the theory of Natural Law.

3. "Human beings are born with the tendency to pursue morally good ends". Evaluate in the light of teleological aspects of Natural Law.

4. " Explain and justify the doctrine of double effect with reference to an ethical dilemma of your choice concerning euthanasia".

Key Quotes - Natural Law

1. "The natural law is the sharing in the eternal law by intelligent creatures". Thomas Aquinas

2. "For Aquinas, the basis of the moral life is prudence, right practical reason in the pursuit of charity". Herbert McCabe

3. "The order of the precepts of the natural law is the order of our natural inclinations". Thomas Aquinas

4. "Our ultimate end is unrelated good, namely God, who alone can fill our will to the brim because of infinite goodness". Thomas Aquinas

5. "The natural law is unchangeable in its first principles, but in its secondary principles it may be changed through some special causes hindering the following of the primary precepts". Thomas Aquinas

6. "The natural law involves universality as it is inscribed in the rational nature of a person. It makes itself felt in every person endowed with reason". Veritatis Splendor (1995)

7. "Every marital act must of necessity retain its intrinsic relationship to the procreation of human life". Humanae Vitae (1968)

8. "The theory of Natural law suggests morality is autonomous. It has its own questions, its own methods of answering them and its own standards of truth. Religious considerations are not the point". James Rachels

9. "The world is conceived as a rational order with value and purpose built into its very nature". James Rachels

10. "Nature inclines to that which is necessary for the perfection of community". Thomas Aquinas

Confusions - Natural Law

1. "Natural" means "as we see in the natural world". This isn't true because many things we see in the natural world we would argue are immoral (eg killing the weak which animals do all the time). "Natural" means something closer to "**APPROPRIATE** for our rational human nature", for example, we may naturally feel lust but it is irrational and wrong to seek to indulge this lust with a complete stranger.

2. "Natural law is dogmatic and inflexible". This is a wrong reading of Aquinas who himself argues that the **SECONDARY PRECEPTS** are liable to change with circumstances and our developed understanding. It is quite possible to be a Natural Law theorist and argue in favour of contraception on the grounds that it is necessary to save lives and reduce destructive population growth. Roman Catholic interpretations are open to debate.

3. "Natural Law is deontological". This is an overstatement as Natural Law is profoundly teleological in its goal of eudaimonia and follows the Greek teleological wordlview. However, it is still law, and is enshrined in principles and rules and codes of law which should reflect the **ETERNAL LAW** of God. The laws have to be **JUST** and subject to right reason.

4. "Natural Law requires God". Aquinas rejects **DIVINE COMMAND THEORY** (the argument that something is gcod or bad because God commands it). Natural Law therefore does not require God but is knowable by reason alone and observable in nature. Christian Natural Law theory argues that the divine blueprint for the Universe is reflected in its design and discoverable by scientific research, as well as reflection on the proper rational purposes of human beings.

Kantian Ethics

Key Terms

- **AUTONOMY** freedom to reason about the moral law

- **CATEGORICAL** unconditional, absolute, with no 'ifs"

- **HYPOTHETICAL** conditional, relative to circumstances, with 'ifs'

- **SUMMUM BONUM** the greatest good, combining virtue and happiness

- **DUTY** the sole moral motive of pursuing a line of action because it is right, whether or not we feel like it

Deontological

A **NORMATIVE** theory (tells you what is right and wrong/what you ought to do), that is **DEONTOLOGICAL** (acts are intrinsically right and wrong in themselves, stressing rules and duties), **ABSOLUTIST** (applies universally in all times, places, situations) and is **A PRIORI** (derived from reason alone, not experience).

Autonomy

The key Kantian assumption is that we are **AUTONOMOUS** moral agents (self-ruled) which have free choice and free reason, rather than **HETERONOMOUS** meaning "ruled by others", where the others could be God, your peer group, or the Church. Kant adopted the **ENLIGHTENMENT** slogan "dare to reason" and was awakened out of his slumbers by reading Jean-Jacques **ROUSSEAU**'s theory of the social contract.

Good Will

Kant argues that the only thing that is morally good without exception is the **GOOD WILL**. A person of good will is someone motivated by **DUTY** alone. They are not motivated by self-interest, happiness or a feeling of sympathy. The good will is an **INTRINSIC** good (it is good in itself and not as a means to something else) and it doesn't matter if it doesn't bring about good consequences. Even if the good will achieved nothing good – even if it were combined with all manner of other evils – "it would shine forth like a jewel, having full value in itself". He contrasts this with other qualities (such as courage) which **CAN** be good but might also be bad depending on the situation (eg a courageous suicide bomber) which are **EXTRINSIC** goods as they depend on the circumstances.

Duty

Kant argues that we must follow our duty. It is not about what we want to do (our **INCLINATIONS**) or what will lead to the best consequences: only the action which springs from duty is a moral action. Doing your duty (eg helping a beggar) may be pleasurable, but this cannot be the reason why you did your duty (the **MOTIVE**). For it to be moral you have to act because it is your duty, and **FOR NO OTHER REASON**.

Categorical Imperative (C.I.)

How do you know what your duty is? Kant argues that this comes from the **CATEGORICAL IMPERATIVE**. It is categorical because it applies to us universally – simply because we have rational wills. By contrast a **HYPOTHETICAL IMPERATIVE** takes the form "If you want X, then you must do Y" (eg if you want to lose weight, then you must stop eating so much). The difference is the categorical imperative applies to us unconditionally, without any reference to a goal we might have (it is simply the form "You must do Y").

C.I. 1 THE FORMULA OF LAW

"So act that the maxim of your action may be willed as a universal law for all humanity". For any action to be moral, you must be able to **CONSISTENTLY UNIVERSALISE** it. For example, if you decide not to keep a promise, then you must be able to consistently imagine a world where **EVERYONE** doesn't keep their promises – something Kant thought was impossible (because then no-one would believe a promise and so promise-keeping would vanish). He calls this a **CONTRADICTION IN NATURE** because the very nature of the thing – promising – is destroyed and so the action becomes self-contradictory.

C.I. 2 FORMULA OF ENDS

"Never treat people simply as a means to an end but always also as an end in themselves". People are **RATIONAL** and **AUTONOMOUS** (self-legislators) and so are worthy of respect. We cannot ONLY use them as a means for getting something else, but always as rational beings with dignity. We universalise our common humanity – which means we treat others as equals, with rights.

C.I.3 FORMULA OF AUTONOMY

Kant imagines a community of purely rational agents, each of whom is a **LEGISLATOR** (someone who decides laws) and a **SUBJECT** (someone who has to follow those laws) in what he calls a **KINGDOM OF ENDS**. We can only act on moral laws that would be accepted by this fully rational community – we belong to a moral parliament where we are free participators in the law-making process. This introduces an important **SOCIAL** aspect to Kantian ethics. "Kantian ethics is the ethics of democracy". James Rachels

Summum Bonum

The **SUMMUM BONUM** or "supreme good" is **VIRTUE** (a person of 'good will' who follows their duty by applying the Categorical Imperative) combined with **HAPPINESS**. We should not act in order to get happiness (because moral action should only involve doing our duty for duty's sake), but the ideal is that we should be happy to the degree that we **DESERVE** to be happy. This is obviously not something that can be found in this life – we see bad people living happy lives and good people living unhappy lives – therefore the Summum Bonum must be able to be achieved in the **AFTERLIFE**.

Three Postulates

Kant argued there are three necessary postulates (or propositions) for morality:

1. **FREEDOM** (we must be free to make moral decisions)

2. **IMMORTALITY** (there must be an afterlife in order to achieve the summum bonum).

3. **GOD** (necessary to guarantee the moral law and to judge fairly and reward or punish).

Strengths Of Kant

It's **REASONABLE** – pretty much what most people consider morality to be about (ie universalising your behaviour). The various formulations of the Categorical Imperative take the **DIGNITY** and **EQUALITY** of human beings very seriously. The innocent are protected by the universal equality given to all human beings.

Weaknesses

It is **INFLEXIBLE** as absolutes have to be applied in all situations irrespective of what we consider to be the wisest choice. Kant also seems to make a clear distinction between our **EMOTIONS** and the ethical choice done from duty alone - but is it really morally doubtful if I act out of emotion like compassion and not just from **DUTY** alone? Also, what happens when two duties **CONFLICT** (eg I need to lie to a crazy knifeman who is enquiring if my friend is in the house - Kant's own example where he insists we tell the truth whatever happens). Surely **CONSEQUENCES** do matter, and arguably there has to be a consequential element to Kant when we imagine universalising an imperative.

Possible Exam Questions

1. "Kantian ethics is not helpful in providing practical guidelines for making moral decisions". Discuss

2. Evaluate to what extent duty can be the sole basis for a moral action.

3. "Kantian ethics is too abstract to be useful in practical ethical decision-making'. Discuss

4. "In neglecting the role of emotions in favour of pure reason, Kantian ethics fails to give a realistic account for our human nature". Discuss

Key Quotes - Kant

1. "It is impossible to conceive of anything in the world good without qualification except the good will". Immanuel Kant

2. "Two things fill me with wonder, the starry hosts above and the moral law within". Immanuel Kant

3. "Kant places the stern voice of duty at the heart of the moral life". Robert Arrington

4. "If our moral sense were based merely on feelings, it would not only vary from person to person – just as some gentlemen prefer blondes and others don't – but could also vary within a person according to his state of health and experiences". Peter Rickman

5. "There remain the categorical imperatives, which derive their authority from reason itself; and the only thing reason abstracted from actual information about specific conditions can command is consistency." Peter Rickman

6. "The highest created good is a world where rational beings are happy and worthy of happiness". Immanuel Kant

7. "To have any goal of action is an act of freedom". Immanuel Kant

8. "With sufficient ingenuity almost every precept can be consistently universalised". Alasdair MacIntyre

9. "There is more to the moral point of view than being willing to universalise one's rules". William Frankena

Confusions - Kant

1. "Duty means blind obedience". This is what Adolf Eichmann implied in his trial in 1962 - but it's not Kant's view of duty which involves reasoning through the **UNIVERSALISABILITY** of your action and treating all human beings with equal respect.

2. "Duty means ignoring emotion". This is a possible reading of Kant, but not the only one. Another reading is to say that Kant saw duty as the primary motive and so long as emotions don't conflict with duty then having moral emotions is fine - just don't base your reason on emotion as it is unreliable.

3. 'Kantian ethics is deontological". William Frankena classified Kant as deontological and it is true Kant argues for unconditional commands (categoricals). But when we universalise we can't help thinking about consequences - there is a consequential dimension to Kant. Whether we have done our duty from the right motive is deontological - but determining the right duty needs a **TELEOLOGICAL** approach.

Bentham's Act Utilitarianism

Key Terms

- **PLEASURE** the one intrinsic good, according to Bentham

- **GREATEST HAPPINESS PRINCIPLE** to act to maximise the greatest happiness of the greatest number - the fundamental principle of utilitarian ethics

- **HEDONIC CALCULUS** a way of quantifying pleasure by seven criteria

- **TELEOLOGICAL** a theory which relates goodness to ends or purposes

- **CONSEQUENTIALIST** identifying goodness by the results of an action

- **EMPIRICAL** a scientific word implying morality can be tested and measured

Background

BENTHAM (1748-1832) was a social reformer who believed that the law should serve human needs and welfare. Where **JUSTICE** was **RETRIBUTIVE** he wanted to see it REFORMING and acting as a **DETERRENCE** – there had to be a real social benefit outweighing the pain to the criminal, and with a better **DISTRIBUTION** of resources, but all in the cause of the **GREATEST HAPPINESS PRINCIPLE (GHP)** –

the motive was to reduce suffering and increase happiness for everyone. The theory is **TELEOLOGICAL** because it measures likely consequences of **ACTIONS**, and **HEDONIC** because Bentham believed pleasure (Greek: hedon) was the key motive and could be quantified. So there is an **EMPIRICAL**, objective measure of goodness.

Motivation

There is one **MORAL** good – pleasure, and one evil – pain. "Nature has placed mankind under two **SOVEREIGN** masters, pain and pleasure". Right actions are on balance pleasurable, wrong actions are on balance painful. Bentham's is therefore a theory of **PSYCHOLOGICAL HEDONISM** (Hedonism - pleasure-seeking).

Hedonic Calculus

The **HEDONIC CALCULUS** is a way of measuring pleasure and pain, so the consequences of an act can be assessed as a score in units of happiness called **HEDONS** (plus for pleasure, minus for pain). The seven criteria are (acronym **PRRICED**): **P**urity, **R**ichness, **R**eliability, **I**ntensity, **C**ertainty, **E**xtent, **D**uration. In this assessment "everyone is to count as one and no-one as more than one" (Bentham), so there is strict **EQUALITY**.

Quantitative Pleasure

Bentham believed "pushpin is as good as poetry" (pushpin – a pub game = playing a slot machine in today's terms). Pleasure is purely **QUANTITATIVE** so we can't award more hedons to listening to Mozart or painting a picture or grasping philosophy. Mill, who was saved from mental breakdown by **WORDSWORTH**'s poetry, really objected to this. According to Bentham, we can compare a small child's delight in a new toy with someone else's delight in a new girlfriend. A **PIG** enjoying a good wallow is of more value than **SOCRATES** having a sightly sad think. Hence "the pig philosophy".

Pleasure Machines

JCC SMART (1973:18-21) asks us to imagine a pleasure machine where we can be wired up every day and passively enjoy every pleasure imaginable (note-addiction often operates like this as a kind of refuge in a supposed pleasure - like drink). **ALDOUS HUXLEY** wrote of a brave new world where people popped **SOMA** tablets to make them happy (there were 41m antidepressant prescriptions last year in the UK). Bentham can have no problems with this, but **MILL** saw happiness as a wider idea involving **ACTIVITY**, and realistic goals and expectations (closer to what my therapist might advise or what **ARISTOTLE** argues).

Strengths - Bentham

There is a **SIMPLICITY** in Bentham's calculation, and a radical **EQUALITY**. The **TELOS** of increasing human welfare is attractive and **COMMON SENSE**. His ideas drove **SOCIAL REFORM** – and he designed a more humane prison called a **PANOPTICON** – never built in the UK, but in Barcelona. There is a lack of snobbery in his classification of all pleasures as **EQUALLY VALID** – why should Mozart be thought better than Rap music (at least in giving pleasure)?

The labels on the Hedon-o-meter, from top to bottom: purity, remoteness, reproducability, intensity, certainty, extent, duration.

HEDON-O-METER

JERRY BENTHAM'S 12 FRUIT SLURPER

Weaknesses

Bentham focuses only on **ACTIONS** so we have to keep on calculating (he doesn't allow us to have **RULES** to make life easier). He equates **PLEASURE** with **HAPPINESS** – but they don't seem to be equivalent (ask the athlete training for the Olympics whether the toil is pleasurable – but it doesn't mean a lack of contentment with training). We can always ask "you're going to the nightclub, but is that a **GOOD** idea?" (Good meaning "promoting your welfare"). Bentham implies pleasure is **MEASURABLE** (it isn't - how can we compare my hedon with yours?). Finally, he has no answer for Smart's **PLEASURE MACHINE** or Huxley's **SOMA** tablet (of course, they were writing two centuries later so even if his stuffed skeleton, residing in a cupboard in London University, could talk, we don't know what it would say!).

Key Quotes - Bentham

1. "Nature has placed mankind under two sovereign masters, pain and pleasure. It is for them to point out what we ought to do as well as determine what we should do". Jeremy Bentham, Principles of Morals

2. "In every human breast, self-regarding interest is predominant over social interest; each person's own individual interest over the interests of all other persons taken together". Jeremy Bentham, Book of Fallacies, p 392

3. "The community is a fictitious body," and it is but "the sum of the interests of the several members who compose it". Jeremy Bentham, Principles of Morals

4. "Prejudice apart, the game of pushpin is of equal value with the arts and sciences of music and poetry. If the game of pushpin furnishes more pleasure, it is more valuable than either". Jeremy Bentham, Principles of Morals

Mill's Rule Utilitarianism

Key Terms

- **ACT UTILITARIANISM** (AU) measuring the utility of an individual act

- **RULE UTILITARIANISM** (RU) focusing on the rules which maximise social happiness

- **RIGHTS** legal obligations which maximise social utility

- **JUSTICE** certain principles, practices and rights which according to Mil guarantee social utility

- **QUALITATIVE PLEASURE** pleasure can be evaluated according to its social value as 'higher' (intellectual) and 'lower' (bodily)

Weak Rule Utilitarianism

The weak **RULE UTILITARIANISM** of John Stuart Mill (1806-73) is a **TELEOLOGICA**L (telos = goal) theory based on a definition of goodness as the **BALANCE** of happiness over misery.

This is a measurable, **EMPIRICAL** idea – measure the happiness effects of likely consequences – giving an **OBJECTIVE** measure of goodness.

Mill was against the **INTUITIONISTS** which he found too **SUBJECTIVE**. Mill argues that happiness is most likely to be maximised by generally following a set of **RULES** which society has found, by experience, maximise utility. But the rules can develop and in cases of moral dilemmas, we should revert to being **ACT UTILITARIANS** (so weak **RU**).

Mill & Bentham

Mill disliked three aspects of **BENTHAM**'s version.

1. The swinish implications of categorising all pleasures as of equal value – drinking beer v. listening to Mozart.

2. The emphasis on pleasure alone, as Mill was influenced by **ARISTOTLE**'s views on virtue (eg the importance of **SYMPATHY** for others).

3. The problem of **JUSTICE** and **RIGHTS** – how do we prevent one innocent person or group being sacrificed for the general happiness of the majority? So Mill devotes the last chapter of his essay to **JUSTICE**.

Mill On Happiness

Mill's definition of a happy life has three elements – pleasure (varied and rich) and absence of pain, **AUTONOMY** (the free choice of a life goal), and **ACTIVITY** (motivated by virtues like sympathy eg Mill used to hand out leaflets advising about contraception and campaigned for women's rights).

"**HAPPINESS** is not a life of rapture, but moments of such, in an existence with few and transitory pains, many and various pleasures, with a decided predominance of the **ACTIVE** over the passive, and having as a foundation of the whole, not to expect more from life than it is capable of bestowing". JS Mill, Utilitarianism

Higher And Lower Pleasures

Mill was saved from a nervous breakdown in his 20s by the **ROMANTIC MOVEMENT** eg Wordsworth's Lyrical Ballads. To him poetry was infinitely superior to **PUSHPIN** (a pub game). So "better to be Socrates dissatisfied than a fool satisfied". T

he **LOWER** bodily pleasures (food, sex, drink, football) were of less value than the **HIGHER** pleasures (reading, thinking, listening to Mozart).

So Mill followed **ARISTOTLE** in seeing education as of vital importance (the supreme Greek value is **CONTEMPLATION** to gain wisdom). Only a person who'd experienced both could really judge the difference in **QUALITY** (so we say qualitative pleasure is superior to quantitative). He called those who hadn't experienced both "inferior beings". Does this make Mill a snob?

Rules

Mill has been called an "inconsistent utilitarian" (Alasdair MacIntyre) – because as his essay goes on he moves from **ACT** to **RULE** utilitarianism. We use generations of past experience to form rules, so we don't have to do a calculation to know whether murder or theft is "right". We inherit **BELIEFS** "and the beliefs which have thus come down are the **RULES** of morality for the multitude" (JS Mill). These are not fixed but "admit of continual improvement" – so not **ABSOLUTE**.

The **FIRST PRINCIPLE** is utility (or the Greatest Happiness Principle) and then **SECONDARY PRINCIPLES** (rules) come from this and are constantly evaluated against the first principle. Just as navigation is based on astronomy (Mill's own analogy) doesn't mean the sailor goes back to the stars every time – no he uses an **ALMANAC** – so, argues Mill, human beings follow a code book of rules passed down from previous generations as the best way to be happy.

But if the depth sounder disagrees with the chart datum (rules of past chart-plotter's experience) we revert to being act utilitarians (my analogy).

Justice

Bernard **WILLIAMS** argued that Utilitarianism violates our **MORAL INTEGRITY** by encouraging us to do things we would find repulsive – like his example of Jim who is invited to kill one Indian as an honoured guest in order to save nineteen others. This is the problem of **INJUSTICE** – the Southern States may have enjoyed lynching innocent people in the 1920s but this doesn't make it right.

Mill argues that unhappiness is caused by selfishness, by people "acting only for themselves", and that for a person to be happy they need "to cultivate a fellow feeling with the collective interests of mankind" and "in the **GOLDEN RULE** of Jesus we find the whole ethics of utility" (JS Mill).

So we need to defend personal **RIGHTS** and "Justice is a name for certain moral requirements, which, regarded collectively, stand higher in the scale of **SOCIAL UTILITY**, and are therefore of more paramount obligation, than any others", and " justice is a name for certain classes of **MORAL RULES**, which concern the essentials of human well-being".

Rights, justice and the virtue of sympathy stop selfish self-interest destroying the happiness of others. So we escape the problem of Jim and the Indians.

Act Or Rule?

LOUIS POJMAN argues (2006:111) that we can adopt a **MULTILEVEL** approach (this is what Mill seems to be doing in talking about **PRIMARY** and **SECONDARY** principles). So we can have three levels if we wish: rules of thumb to live by which generally maximise utility, a second set of rules for resolving conflicts between these, and a third process – an **ACT** utilitarian one, for assessing a difficult situation according to the Greatest Happiness Principle (eg lying to save a friend). But in this way philosophers like **J.O.URMSON** argue that **RULE** utilitarianism collapses into **ACT** utilitarianism. Mill might counter that we don't have the time, the wisdom, or the resources to keep calculating every action and this multilevel approach is therefore realistic and practical in a way that **KANT**'s deontology is unrealistic and impractical because it cannot handle **MORAL DILEMMAS**.

Strengths

RATIONALITY and **PRACTICALITY** Utilitarian ethics rests on a rational calculation of numbers of people whose pleasure or happiness is maximised. There is a clarity and simplicity to this.

EQUALITY is central. Bentham wrote "everyone is to count as one, and no-one as more than one". This radical idea implies that everyone has equal weight in the utility calculation.

MILL adds equal **RIGHTS**. Suppose, on an equal vote, you all vote for my dismissal (or even death) in line with maximising general happiness? Mill argues this sort of law would violate rights and such a society would not be one that we'd choose to live in - it would be miserable. "The utilitarian emphasis on impartiality must be a part of any defensible moral theory". (Rachels, 2006:114). Finally, utilitarianism takes account of the **FUTURE** – issues of climate change, potential future wars and famines all suggest we need an ethical theory that takes into account those yet unborn.

Weaknesses

MOTIVE, "why should I maximise pleasure or happiness?" We can't agree how to define pleasure or happiness. Bentham and Mill don't notice the difficulty of the concept of "pleasure" a fatal objection at the outset", Anscombe (1958:2). Then there is a difficulty in making me think of the interests (happiness) of others. Mill tries to bring "sympathy" in as a kind of virtue or psychological motive.

DISTRIBUTION problems emerge when I try to maximise **TOTAL** not **AVERAGE** happiness – eg low tax for the rich may raise the total but reduce average happiness, because the 10% super rich are much, much happier.

Finally **CONSEQUENCES** are hard to calculate if you don't have the omniscience of God. The **IRAQ WAR** may have seemed justifiable by the Greatest Happiness Principle - but looking with hindsight we might argue - better a Saddam Hussein in power than a million deaths?

Possible Exam Questions

1. Evaluate the view that utilitarianism does not provide a helpful way of solving moral dilemmas.

2. "The application of the greatest happiness principle in specific situations is not a sufficient guide to the good action". Discuss

3. "Pleasure is not quantifiable". Discuss

4. To what extent does utilitarian ethics provide a useful guide to issues surrounding business ethics?

Key Quotes - Mill's Utilitarianism

1. "It is better to be a human being dissatisfied than a pig satisfied; better Socrates dissatisfied than a fool satisfied". J.S.Mill, Utilitarianism

2. "Happiness is...moments of rapture...in an existence of few and transitory pains, many and various pleasures, with a predominance of the active over the passive..not to expect more from life than it is capable of bestowing". J.S. Mill, Utilitarianism

3. "Whatever we adopt as the fundamental principle of Morality refers to the first-order beliefs and practices about good and evil by means of which we guide our behaviour. For morality, we require subordinate principles to apply it by". (Fundamental principle = happiness is good, subordinate principles = rules) J.S. Mill, Utilitarianism

4. "By the improvement of education, the feeling of unity with our fellow-creatures shall be as deeply rooted in our character, as the horror of crime is in an ordinarily well brought up young person". (= sympathy) JS Mill, Utilitarianism

5. "To have a right, then, is, I conceive, to have something which society should defend me in possession of. If the objector asks why? I can give no other answer than general utility". J.S.Mill, Utilitarianism

6. "Justice is a name for certain moral requirements, which, regarded collectively, stand higher in the scale of social utility, than any others". J.S.Mill, Utilitarianism

7. "I account the justice which is grounded on utility to be the chief part, and incomparably the most sacred and binding part, of all morality." J.S.Mill, Utilitarianism

8. "Because our relation to the world is partly given by moral feelings, and by a sense of what we can or cannot "live with", to regard those feelings....as happening outside one's moral self is to lose one's moral identity; to lose one's integrity". (Bernard Williams, Utilitarianism For and Against pg 104)

9. "In the golden rule of Jesus of Nazareth we find the whole ethics of utility". JS Mill, Utilitarianism

Confusions - Mill

1. Was Mill an Act or Rule Utilitarian? He is sometimes described as a **WEAK RULE UTILITARIAN**. Mill believed that generally we should follow the rule as this reflects society's view of what maximises happiness from past social experience. But when a pressing utilitarian need arises we should break the rule and so become an act utilitarian.

2. "Mill took Bentham's view that happiness equates to pleasure". Sometimes Mill seems to argue this, but it's truer to say Mill's view is close to **ARISTOTLE**'s that happiness means "personal and social flourishing". So to Mill the individual cannot be happy without the guarantee of certain rules and rights and clear goals to aim for.

3. "Utilitarianism ignores individual rights". Mill would vigorously deny this: rights are essential for the happy society and the happy society generally, with a sense of security, is essential for happy individuals. However, a Benthamite view of individual **ACT UTILITARIANISM** is subject to this criticism (as is US foreign policy which included Guantanamo Bay and Rendition), because many people's pleasure outweighs one or two people's pain (it's the **BALANCE** of pleasure over pain that matters morally).

4. "Utilitarianism is a form of egoism". Utilitarianism escapes this criticism for two reasons: there is an impartiality as "everyone to count as one" and secondly, because the virtue of **SYMPATHY** as a moral feeling is fundamental to my concern for your welfare.

Situation Ethics - Christian Relativism

Situation Ethics is a **NORMATIVE** theory (tells you what is right/wrong – what you ought to do), that is **TELEOLOGICAL** and **CONSEQUENTIALIST** (acts are right or wrong if they bring about good/bad consequences, or can be seen as instrumentally good/bad) and **RELATIVIST** (there are no universal rules as actions depend on circumstances; there is just one general universal value – that of agape love). It is also **CHRISTIAN**, based on the principle of sacrificial love (**AGAPE**).

Introduction

Joseph Fletcher (1966) argued there are three approaches to ethics:

1. **LEGALISTIC** – someone who follows absolute rules and laws. Fletcher rejects this as it leads to **UNTHINKING OBEDIENCE** and needs elaborate systems of exceptions and compromises.

2. **ANTINOMIAN** – (nomos is Greek for law, so anti-law) or someone who rejects all rules and laws (Fletcher rejects this as it would lead to social **CHAOS**).

3. **SITUATIONAL** – Fletcher argues that each individual situation is different and absolute rules are too demanding and restrictive. Instead we should decide what is the most **LOVING** course of

action (**AGAPE**). The Situationist has respect for laws and tradition, but they are only guidelines to how to achieve this loving outcome, and thus they may be broken if the other course of action would result in more love.

However, Situation Ethics is not **FULLY** relativist: it has an absolute principle (love) that is non-negotiable.

Origins Of Agape In The New Testament

William Temple wrote "there is only one ultimate and invariable duty; and its formula is this: "thou shalt love thy neighbour as thyself" (1917:206). He went on: "what acts are right depends on circumstances" (1934:405). Fletcher was inspired by Temple but also argues that love is the fundamental controlling norm. There is a case for arguing this from the New Testament.

- Love is the heart of God's **CHARACTER**. "God is love" (1 John 4:8). This echoes the Old Testament description of God as one "abounding in steadfast love and faithfulness" (Exodus, 34:8) in his revelation to Moses.

- Love is the fulfilling of the **LAW**. Love interprets the commandments and allows us sometimes to break them. In John 8 Jesus refuses to allow them to stone an adulterous woman in direct breach of Leviticus 20:10.

- Love is the heart of a controlling **PARABLE** of the Good Samaritan., (Luke 10). "Controlling" in the sense that Jesus' own sacrificial love mirrors that of the outsider who did all he could to help the victim, as priests and officials passed by, and so the parable 'controls' our interpretation of the entire mission of Christ.

- Love is Jesus' new **COMMAND** (John 13:34) - 'a new commandment I give to you to love one another as I have loved you".

- Sacrificial love (**AGAPE**) is the highest form of love; "Greater love has no man than this, that he lay down his life for his friends". John 15:13

- Love is also the supreme **VIRTUE** in the writings of Paul, with many characteristics (kindness, patience, forgiveness, positivity, hopefulness, perserverance), (1 Corinthians 13).

- Love is given to us by the **SPIRIT** of love, says Paul - the Holy Spirit. (Romans 5:5)

So although the Greeks had several words for love - friendship, family love, erotic love - the greatest moral value is given to **AGAPE**.

Four Working Principles

In Situation Ethics there are **FOUR WORKING PRINCIPLES** (Fletcher's own term).

1. **PRAGMATISM** – (what you propose must be practical – work in practice).

2. **RELATIVISM** – (there are no fixed, absolute rules – all decisions are relative to **AGAPE** love. If love demands that you steal food, then you should steal food. Notice this is special meaning of relativism - Fletcher calls his theory 'principled relativism' because every action is made relative to the one principle of agape love.

3. **POSITIVISM** – (Kant and Natural Law are based on reason as both theories argue reason can uncover the right course of action). Fletcher disagrees with this: you have to start with a **POSITIVE** choice or commitment – you need to want to do good. There is no rational answer to the question "why should I love?" We accept this norm by faith.

4. **PERSONALISM** – (people come first: you cannot sacrifice people to rules or laws)

Six Fundamental Principles

1. Nothing is good in itself except **LOVE** (it is the only thing that is absolutely good, the only thing with intrinsic value).

2. Jesus replaced the law with love or **AGAPE** ("The ruling norm of Christian decision is love, nothing else". Joseph Fletcher).

3. Love and **JUSTICE** are the same thing (if love is put into practice it can only result in fair treatment and fair distribution).

4. Love desires the good of **OTHERS** (it does not have favourites, but this doesn't mean we have to **LIKE** them).

5. Only the **END JUSTIFIES THE MEANS** (if an action causes harm, it is wrong. If good comes of it, it is right).

6. Love's decisions are made in each **SITUATION**.

Conscience

Fletcher argues conscience has many potential meanings:

- **THE VOICE OF GOD** - as in the writings of Cardinal John Henry Newman.

- **PRACTICAL REASON** or phronesis - one of two meanings in the writings of Thomas Aquinas.

- **AN INSTINCT** we are born with. Aquinas' other word for conscience is **SYNDERESIS,** meaning an innate conscience.

- **AS A VERB** - Fletcher rejects the idea of conscience as a 'faculty' and argues it is like a verb reflecting our actions in doing loving things: 'there is no conscience; 'conscience' is merely a word for our attempts to make decisions creatively, constructively, fittingly'. (1966:53)

Strengths Of Situation Ethics

It takes **INDIVIDUALS** and their needs seriously. It's also **FLEXIBLE** and also allows us to make judgements in situations where two moral principles conflict. **LOVE** is an important value somewhat neglected by other theories, as the motive of sympathy in Mill's utilitarian ethics is not quite as strong as the **AGAPE** of Joseph Fletcher.

Weaknesses Of Situation Ethics

LOVE is a very demanding value to place at the centre of your ethics - can anyone love sacrificially all the time? Mustn't we be selfish some of the time? Like all **CONSEQUENTIALIST** theories it's impossible to calculate into the future making this particular love calculation **IMPOSSIBLE**. William Barclay argues that Fletcher fails to realise the value of law - as an expression fo the collective wisdom of generations before us, so the moral law is a guide which we shouldn't throw away so easily. Law also defines the **FABRIC** of society.

Possible Exam Questions

1. "Situation ethics is too demanding as a system of ethical decision-making". Discuss

2. "Goodness is only defined by asking - how is agape best served". Discuss

3. "Agape is not so much a religious idea as an equivalent to saying 'I want the best for you'". Discuss

4. Evaluate the extent to which situation ethics is individualistic and subjective.

Key Quotes - Situation Ethics

1. "Love alone is always good and right in every situation". Joseph Fletcher (Situation Ethics, 1966:69)

2. "Faith, hope and love abide, these three, but the greatest of all is love". 1 Corinthians 13:13

3. "God is love". 1 John 4:8

4. "A new commandment I give to you, that you love one another". John 13:34

5. "Love your neighbour as yourself". Jesus replied, 'Go and do likewise". Luke 10:27,28

6. "There can be and often is a conflict between law and love". Joseph Fletcher (1966:70)

7. "Too much law means the obliteration of the individual; too much individualism means a weakening of the law...there is a place for law as the encourager of morality". William Barclay, Ethics in a Permissive Society p189

8. In 1952 **POPE PIUS XII** called situation ethics "an individualistic and subjective appeal to the concrete circumstances of actions to justify decisions in opposition to the **NATURAL LAW** or God's revealed will'.

9. "High authority has held that a starving man should rather steal a loaf than die of hunger". William Temple (referring to Aquinas)

10. "Every moral act must be good or evil by reason of some circumstance". Thomas Aquinas (de Malo; Q2 A5c)

Some Possible Confusions

1. "Situation ethics is a form of relativism". Fletcher denies this as he argues it is 'principled relativism' - meaning that the supreme norm of love is applied to situations and made relative to need and circumstances. There is thus one absolute norm - **AGAPE.** This is not relativism in the sense of the denial of objective truth, it is relativism in the sense of 'goodness is relative to the situation' (a relativism of application not of norms).

2. "Situation ethics is a religious ethic". It is true that **AGAPE** is a controlling norm of the **NEW TESTAMENT**. Also the parable of the Good Samaritan (Luke 10) appears to be a form of situationism 'go and do likewise', says Jesus, which seems to mean 'go and work out love in the situations you find yourself'. When Fletcher gave up Christianity he still argued that the non-Christian will equate goodness with an idea such as Aristotle's **EUDAIMONIA** (flourishing) whereas the Christian would always maintain **AGAPE** as the supreme norm. So there may be a difference there between atheistic situationism and religious forms.

3. "Jesus was a situationist". It is true that Jesus overthrows some elements of the **LEVITICAL CODE** of law such as stoning adulterers, the uncleanness of certain types of food (such as pork), the uncleanness of certain types of people (such as menstruating women). It is also true that the parable of the **GOOD SAMARITAN** promotes a situationist ethic. However, he also said "I came not to abolish the law but to fulfil the law" (Matthew 5:17). This implies that the fundamental principles of the law such as justice, truth and equality are perfectly fufilled in Jesus, even if he rejects some of the ritualistic practices.

Euthanasia

Definitions

- **EUTHANASIA** (Greek = good death) is the practice of ending life to reduce pain and suffering (so "mercy killing").

- **VOLUNTARY** euthanasia = when a patient's death is caused by another person eg doctor with the **EXPLICIT CONSENT** of the patient. The patient request must be **VOLUNTARY** (acting without coercion, pressure) **ENDURING** (lasts some time or is repeated over time) and **COMPETENT** (they have the mental capacity to choose). A variation on euthanasia is **PHYSICIAN-ASSISTED SUICIDE** – this differs from euthanasia as the doctor will help the patient to commit suicide (eg set up the apparatus), but the final act of killing is done by the patient.

- **NON-VOLUNTARY** euthanasia is done without the patient's consent, because they are not competent or able to give the consent (eg in a coma, on a life support machine). The doctor and/or the family may take the decision. A famous test case was that of **TONY BLAND** who was in a persistent vegetative state following the 1989 Hillsborough football disaster.

- **INVOLUNTARY** euthanasia is performed **AGAINST** the wishes of the patient. This is widely opposed and illegal in the UK.

Active Or Passive

ACTIVE euthanasia is the direct and **DELIBERATE** killing of a patient.

PASSIVE euthanasia is when life-sustaining treatment is withdrawn or withheld.

This distinction may also be described as the difference between an **ACT** and an **OMISSION** (failing to act) and between **KILLING** and **ALLOWING TO DIE**. Some, such as James Rachels, argue there is no real difference – if anything passive euthanasia (withdrawal of treatment) is worse because it leads to a longer, drawn out death and so more suffering potentially. **DAME CICELY SAUNDERS** (who founded the hospice movement) argues that it is unnecessary for anyone to suffer a painful death with modern drugs. A counter-argument is that many doctors already hasten death (eg by doubling a morphine dose): under the doctrine of **DOUBLE EFFECT** (part of Natural Law theory), if the intention is to alleviate pain and a secondary effect to kill someone, the doctor is not guilty of any crime.

Legal Position

Until 1961 suicide was illegal in the UK. The **1961 SUICIDE ACT** legalised suicide but made it illegal to assist.

The **NETHERLANDS** and **SWITZERLAND** allow voluntary euthanasia (active and passive) and physician-assisted suicide. The **DIGNITAS** clinic in Switzerland helped 107 British people to die in 2010. **DR ANNE TURNER** (aged 66) was one such person in 2009 – subject of the docu-drama "A Short Stay in Switzerland". No-one has ever been prosecuted in the UK for helping a relative or friend go to Switzerland.

In 2010 Director of Public Prosecutions **KEIR STARMER** confirmed that relatives of people who kill themselves will not face prosecution as long as they do not maliciously encourage them and assist only a "clear settled and informed wish" to commit suicide. The move came after the Law Lords backed multiple sclerosis sufferer Debbie Purdy's call for a policy statement on whether people who help someone commit suicide should be prosecuted.

Keir Starmer concluded: "There are **NO GUARANTEES** against prosecution and it is my job to ensure that the most vulnerable people are protected while at the same time giving enough information to those people like Mrs Purdy who want to be able to make informed decisions about what actions they may choose to take".

The **OREGON RULES** are another attempt to legalise assisted suicide by laying down conditions under which it will be allowed in US law.

Sanctity Of Life: Bible

The Bible argues that life is a gift from God. Humans are created in the **IMAGE OF GOD** (Genesis 1:27) and the **INCARNATION** (God taking human form – John 1:14) shows the sacred value of human life. Human life is a **GIFT** or **LOAN** from God (Job 1:21 "The Lord gave and the Lord has taken away"). We should also show **RESPECT** for human life: "thou shalt not murder" (Exodus 20:13). We should also "choose life" (Deuteronomy 30). Finally, Christian love (**AGAPE**) is crucial (1 Corinthians 13 "the greatest value of all is love"). We should protect human life (the parable of the Good Samaritan) particularly as God gave his only son to redeem us (bring us back from sin and death) and give us the gift of "life in all its fullness".

Sanctity Of Life

- The **NATURAL LAW** view argues that there is a **PRIMARY PRECEPT** to "preserve life" and views life as an **INTRINSIC** good. Euthanasia is therefore wrong and the Catholic Church forbids both active and passive euthanasia as "contrary to the dignity of the human person and the respect due to God, his creator" (Catechism of the Roman Catholic Church). However, the **DOCTRINE OF DOUBLE EFFECT** might accept the shortening of human life (eg if the intention is to relieve pain, secondary effect to kill) so long as it is only a **FORESEEN BUT UNINTENDED RESULT**. The Catholic Church also makes a distinction between **ORDINARY MEANS** (ordinary, usual medical treatments) and **EXTRAORDINARY MEANS** (treatments that are dangerous, a huge burden, or disproportionate). It is morally acceptable to stop extraordinary means, as "it is the refusal of over-zealous treatment".

- **ROMAN CATHOLIC** version of Natural law: "Discontinuing medical procedures that are burdensome, dangerous, extraordinary, or disproportionate to the expected outcome can be legitimate; it is the refusal of "over-zealous" treatment. Here one does not will to cause death; one's inability to impede it is merely accepted. The decisions should be made by the patient if he is competent and able or, if not, by those legally entitled to act for the patient, whose reasonable will and legitimate interests must always be respected." Catholic Catechism 2278

- **HUMANIST ARGUMENTS** Following Mill's rule utilitarianism, we could argue that a. A general rule should be in place for social happiness prohibiting euthanasia (so the elderly don't feel under pressure or depressed people feel the temptation). But, b. In specific cases near the end of life doctor's using their discretion should hasten death. This is the present UK situation, which can be justified by rule utilitarian (non-Christian) arguments, giving a modified humanist sanctity of life view.

Quality Of Life: Situation Ethics

JAMES RACHELS argues that the sanctity of life tradition places too much value on human life and there are times (eg with abortion and euthanasia) when this is unhelpful. He makes a distinction between **BIOLOGICAL LIFE** ("being alive" = functioning biological organism) and **BIOGRAPHICAL LIFE** ("having a life" = everything that makes us who we are). He says that what matters is biographical life and if this is already over (for example in a **PERSISTENT VEGETATIVE STATE = PVS**), then taking away biological life is acceptable.

PETER SINGER, a preference utilitarian, argues that the worth of human life varies (the value of human life is not a sacred gift but depends on its **QUALITY**). A low quality of life (judged by the patient) can justify them taking their life or justify someone else doing it for them.

SITUATION ETHICS would also take quality of life as more important than sanctity of life. **PERSONALISM** requires we take a case by case approach, and if someone is suffering in extreme discomfort, then **AGAPE** would dictate that we support their euthanasia. There may however be situations where someone is depressed, for example, where the most loving thing is to persuade them of a life worth living. **PRAGMATISM** demands a case by case and flexible approach. Joseph Fletcher was a himself a pioneer in bioethics and argued: "To bring this matter into the open practice of medicine would harmonise the civil law with medical morals, which must be concerned with the quality of life, not merely its quantity."

Autonomy

JOHN STUART MILL (On Liberty, 1859) argues that individuals should have full **AUTONOMY** (the freedom to make decisions without coercion) so long as it does not harm other people. Individuals cannot be compelled to do things for their own good – "over his own mind-body the individual is sovereign". Those who support voluntary euthanasia believe that personal autonomy and self-determination (choosing what happens to you) are crucial. Any competent adult should be able to decide on the time and manner of their death.

KANT assumes autonomy as one of his three key postulates (together with God and immortality). We are self-legislating, free moral beings. However, he argued in an essay on suicide that suicide was self-contradictory as, if it was universalised, the human race would die out.

DIANE PRETTY argued in a court case in 2002 that Article 1 of the Human Rights Convention (the right to life) included the right to take one's own life. This autonomy argument was rejected by the court. She was paralysed by motor-neurone disease and requested permission for her husband to assist her to die.

Arguments Against Euthanasia

PALLIATIVE CARE – Dame Cicely Saunders argues that there is a better alternative for euthanasia in providing a pain-free death for terminally ill patients. The **HOSPICE** movement may be seen as an alternative, BUT this level of care is not available to everyone, is expensive and cannot fully relieve a patient's suffering (eg for someone who cannot breathe unassisted).

VOLUNTARY AND COMPETENT – some raise questions about voluntary euthanasia. Can the patient ever be free from coercion (eg relatives who want an inheritance or doctors who need to free up resources)? Is the patient likely to be competent (eg when under high doses of medication, or when depressed, or senile). Response would be that there are at least some clear cases when patients **ARE** clearly voluntary (not coerced) and competent. Guidelines such as Starmer's or the **OREGON RULES** require a certain time period of repeated requests to different people, which are then independently confirmed.

SLIPPERY SLOPE – this is the argument that once allowed, the outcome will be a process of a further decline in respect for human life and will end with the practice of non-voluntary euthanasia for the elderly seen as "unaffordable" by the working majority. A response might be that there is a clear difference between voluntary and non-voluntary euthanasia. Is there any evidence of a slippery slope in the US state of Oregon or Switzerland? The rules on assisted suicide are drawn up precisely to stop the slide into widespread disrespect for human life. Note this is an **EMPIRICAL, CONSEQUENTIALIST** argument about probabilities.

DOCTOR-PATIENT RELATIONSHIP – some argue that doctors have a duty to preserve life (the **HIPPOCRATIC OATH**). Euthanasia will undermine the trust between patient and doctor if there is a fear that they will seek to end their life. However, as with abortion, there will remain doctors opposed to euthanasia which a patient could always choose, and it is highly unlikely that GPs will have any say in the process of mercy killing.

Some Possible Questions

1. Natural Law is superior to situation ethics in its treatment of issues surrounding euthanasia". Discuss

2. "Autonomy as an ideal is unrealistic. No-one is perfectly autonomous". Discuss with reference to the ethical issue of euthanasia.

3. "Sanctity of human life is the core principle of medical ethics". Discuss

4. "There is no moral difference between actively ending a life by euthanasia and omitting to treat the patient". Discuss

Key Quotes

1. "Euthanasia is contrary to the dignity of the human person and the respect due to God, His creator". Roman Catholic Catechism

2. "The Lord gave, and the Lord takes away; blessed be the name of the Lord". Job 1:21

3. "God created man in His own image". Genesis 1:27

4. "God knit you together in your mother's womb". Psalm 139:6

5. "Discontinuing medical procedures that are burdensome, dangerous, or disproportionate to the expected outcome can be legitimate". Catholic Catechism

6. "Compare a severely defective human infant with a nonhuman animal, we will often find the non-human to have superior capacities". Peter Singer

7. "We see a life of permanent coma as in no way preferable to death". Jonathan Glover

8. "The ability to make complex judgements about benefit requires compassion, experience and an appreciation of the patient's viewpoint". British Medical Association

9. "Once the boundary is crossed it is hard to see how social and commercial pressures do not define the 'volunteers'." Alastair Campbell in Gill, R. ed Euthanasia and the Churches (Cassell, 1998 p 94)

10. 'For all too many people there are good and reasonable grounds for the deepest despair. Where suffering is reasonably perceived to be unbearable, suicide can be morally right". James Gustafson Ethics from a Theocentric Perspective, (Chicago, 1984 p 214)

Business Ethics

Introduction

BUSINESS ETHICS is the critical examination of how people and institutions should behave in the world of commerce e.g. appropriate limits on self-interest, or (for firms) profits, when the actions of individuals or firms affect others. We may examine **CODES** which companies publish, or **BEHAVIOUR** of individuals – but also **CORPORATE CULTURE** (which may contradict the code) and responsibilities to the **ENVIRONMENT** and the developing world created by **GLOBALISATION** of markets and free trade between countries. We are asked to apply the Kantian idea of **UNIVERSALISED** duties and categoricals to business ethics, and utilitarian ideas of calculating net happiness or pleasure. according to **CONSEQUENCES**.

Key Terms

- **PROFIT MOTIVE** - the reward for risk-taking in maximising returns on any investment.

- **STAKEHOLDERS** - any parties affected by a business practice.

- **EXTERNALITIES** - costs or benefits external to the company – pollution is a negative externality.

- **GLOBALISATION** - the interconnection of economies ,

information and culture.

- **MULTINATIONALS** - companies trading in many countries.

Issues

Does the **PROFIT MOTIVE** conflict with ethical practice? Or does good ethics result in good business.

Should the regulation of business be left to **GOVERNMENTS**?

Ben and Jerry's has this **SOCIAL RESPONSIBILITY** statement at its heart: "to operate the company in a way that recognises the role business plays in the wider society and to find innovative ways to improve the life of the wider community". How widely is this view shared?

What happens when **STAKEHOLDER** interests conflict (eg sacking workers to raise shareholder returns?).

In a **GLOBALISED** world should we treat all workers the same irrespective of differences in national laws (think of safety regulations overseas)? Do **MULTINATIONALS** have too much power?

Stake-Holders

A **STAKEHOLDER** is any individual or group who has a stake in the success or failure of a company. It includes **INTERNAL STAKEHOLDERS** (managers, employees) and **EXTERNAL** (the local community, customers, shareholders, suppliers, local authorities,

Government, other countries). For example, the existence of a Tesco store may mean local shopkeepers do better (if more people visit the town) or worse (if business is taken away).

Stakeholder theory suggest we should consider the interests of all stakeholders in the consequences of a decision.

Codes

Most companies have **CODES OF ETHICS** which lay out the rights of different groups and the responsibilities and values of the company. **ETHICAL INVESTORS** only invest in companies that fulfil certain criteria eg **ENVIRONMENTAL** responsibility, and **FAIR TRADE** for overseas workers.

ETHICAL CONSUMERS look for sustainable sources or organic produce. The April 2011 riots in **BRISTOL** against the Tesco local store show how different interests may clash – stakeholders such as local businesses/some customers v. large corporations/ other customers and employees. Does Tesco have an **ETHICAL DUTY** not to destroy local businesses, or a duty to its potential **EMPLOYEES** (jobs) and **CUSTOMERS** (lower prices)? Is there and **ABSOLUTE** principle we can find to judge between them?

Most companies have ethics codes. But do they embody them as virtues?

Cost/Benefit

COST/BENEFIT analysis is a business equivalent to **UTILITARIAN**

ethics, as it seeks to weigh the benefits in money terms of a business decision against the cost. It suffers the same problem: the denial of **INDIVIDUAL RIGHTS** as a moral **ABSOLUTE**.

In the case of **FORD PINTO** (1970s) the cost of a **HUMAN LIFE** was weighed against the number of likely accidents and the cost of a **PRODUCT RECALL**. At $13 a car it was not worth the recall, they decided. But – they didn't calculate **CONSEQUENCES** correctly and valued **HUMAN LIFE** too cheaply – so ended up paying millions in compensation and having to **RECALL** the car anyway.

Unfortunately value has to be placed on a human life in traffic safety, **NHS** budgets etc – it's not economic to place a crash barrier alongside roads adjacent to remote reservoirs – so tragic accidents do occur (e.g in April 2011 four die in a car plunging into a reservoir in Wales).

If environmental costs are too high, will companies pay them or relocate their business?

Externalities

EXTERNALITIES are costs paid (eg pollution) or benefits enjoyed (eg flowers in a roundabout) by someone external to the firm.

Traditionally Governments have taxed and regulated firms to make them comply with their ethical duties: **THE TEN HOURS ACT** (1847 restricts child labour to 10 hrs a day), the **CLEAN AIR ACT** (1956 restricts carbon emissions), the **HEALTH AND SAFETY ACT** (1974 – improved safety standards and penalised non-compliance), the **SEX DISCRIMINATION ACT** (1975 – Equal Pay and opportunity for women).

MILTON FRIEDMAN (economist) argues that companies have a duty only to their shareholders (ie profits) – it is for society to set the other ethical rules. But examples such as **ENRON**, the US energy company that went bankrupt in 2003 after massive fraud, indicate that laws are never enough – individuals need to take **RESPONSIBILITY**.

As environmental regulation increases the cost to companies rises. Yet the USA has still not signed up to immediate carbon emission reduction despite the 1996 **KYOTO** protocol and the **COPENHAGEN** (2008)and **DURBAN** (2011) summits. Although China, Russia and America signed the Durban agreement, this only committed countries to define a future treaty by 2015, which will be binding in 2020.Once again immediate action has been postponed. US Senator Jim Inhofe, who has called climate change "the greatest hoax every perpetrated on the American people", applauded the "complete collapse of the global warming movement and the Kyoto protocol".

Rights

ABSOLUTISTS (eg Kantians) argue for universal human rights that apply everywhere for all time – including workers and communities in third world countries.

Because **GLOBALISATION** includes the free flow of **CAPITAL** to least cost countries, this can include those with corrupt governments or lax health and safety laws. Union Carbide (US firm) plant in **BHOPAL** (1986, India) and **TRAFIGURA** oil waste disposal (2008, Ivory Coast, hydrogen sulphide) illustrate how thousands can die (Bhopal – mustard gas) or go sick (Trafigura) when companies pursue least cost choices to boost **PROFIT**.

Worker and community rights often seem to take second place to **SHAREHOLDER** interests.

Individuals

Individual workers may become **WHISTLEBLOWERS** and expose fraud, corruption, lax standards etc. The RBS sacked their finance director who "didn't fit in" = opposed their lending policy before the **GLOBAL FINANCIAL CRISIS**.

UK banks were 24 hours from collapse in 2008 before a Government rescue plan, in taking on their bad debts. The rescue of **ROYAL BANK OF SCOTLAND** cost £43bn. But in the **EUROZONE** crisis countries act like individuals, with David Cameron vetoing a recent treaty change because of Britain's **NATIONAL INTEREST**. Is there such an idea as **COLLECTIVE** (European) interest?

Individual **CONSCIENCE** may serve the **public good,** but at the cost of their own **SELF-INTEREST** (they're fired). Kantian ethics may help us cling to **ABSOLUTES**, but Utilitarian ethics tends to make us pragmatists as at the **NORMATIVE** level we lie or stay silent to serve a **COLLECTIVE** interest (and we may not have enough sympathy with outsiders to care).

However **ENRON**'s collapse in 2003 brought down auditor **ARTHUR ANDERSEN** as it was implicated in the financial fraud which covered up huge debts, and affected shareholders, employees and pensioners. Sometimes **SHORT -TERMISM** in the utilitarian calculation can have terrible long-term consequences, and the courage of **ERIN BROKOVITCH** in exposing the toxic leaks of **PACIFIC GAS** in an

American town shows how a Kantian sense of duty may have much to teach us in Business affairs, even though it can be risky for an individual to take on powerful corporations.There was one Enron whistleblower - Vice-President Sherron Watkins - but she only blew as far as Chairman Ken Lay.

Future Generations

One of the puzzles of ethics is how we account for the interests of future generations and animals, plants, etc. Both **KANTIAN** and **UTILITARIAN** ethics are traditionally weak on environmental issues (Kant stresses rational autonomous beings as having moral worth, not animals, and utilitarianism sees the environment as having only **INSTRUMENTAL** goodness as a means to human happiness. This may suffer from the problem of **SHORT-TERMISM)**.

UTILITARIANISM however can arguably do better because the long term happiness of the human race is clearly one factor to consider – but how do we know how many people to add in to the calculation? How do we assess the environmental effect of the plastic bag "island" the size of Texas which exists in the central vortex of the **PACIFIC** ocean currents? **SUSTAINABLE DEVELOPMENT** is a new idea – and **CHRISTIAN ETHICS** has arguably suffered from an emphasis on **DOMINION** (Genesis 1:26) = exploit, rather than **STEWARDSHIP** = care for the environment.

Can we provide incentives to this generation to protect future rights of the unborn?

Globalisation

Globalisation is the **INTERCONNECTION** of markets, technology and information across the world. There are said to be five global brands: Nike, Coca-Cola, McDonalds, Levis. However globalisation brings the risk that large companies dominate the political agenda working in their own interest, and also force wages down for third world suppliers. For example, multinationals fund **PRESIDENTIAL** campaigns and the oil industry lobbies ceaselessly to stop any rise in **OIL PRICES** and even, it has been alleged, the development of alternative energy sources.

The economist Amartya Sen has argued that the central issue is "the **UNEQUAL SHARING** in the benefits of globalisation" – that the poor receive an unequal gain from any wealth created. Put another way, less developed countries are exploited for cheap labour in the global market place (compare **WAGES PER HOUR** in China and the UK for example).

Finally there is the question of **REGULATION**. Do multinationals export lax safety standards and poor environmental disciplines to the third world? The examples of **BHOPAL** (1984) and **TRAFIGURA*** (2007) are not encouraging. And could any government have stopped a deregulated world banking system bringing the world economy to the brink of collapse in the crisis of 2008? Short-term profit and excessive **RISK-TAKING** in property lending led to the accumulation of huge debts so that Royal Bank of Scotland was only saved from bankruptcy by a £43bn cash injection by the UK Government.

Are multinationals beyond state regulation? Do they have too much power? What incentive do they have to be ethical?

* In 2007 Trafigura established a foundation to promote environmental concern, rural development programmes and health programmes in the

counties where it operated. So far $ 14.5 m dollars has been donated to 36 projects. It is now seeking to create "a lasting, sustainable model for corporate philanthropy", perhaps trying to counteract the bad publicity generated by the waste dumping scandal.

Possible Exam Questions

1. "Kantian ethic of duty is superior to the utilitarian ethic of happiness in dealing with difficult business decisions". Discuss

2. "Corporate social responsibility is ethical window-dressing to cover their greed". Discuss

3. Evaluate the view that capitalism will always exploit human beings in the pursuit of profit.

4. "Globalisation widens the exploitation of human beings by reducing the need for ethically valid regulation of business behaviour". Discuss

Key Quotes

1. 'Corporate executives do not have responsibilities in their business activities, other than to make as much money as possible for their shareholders" Milton Friedman

2. "Good employees are good people". Robert Solomon

3. "The following duties bind the employer: not to look upon their work people as their slaves, but to respect in every man his dignity as a person ennobled by Christian character". Rerum Novarum 1891(p 20)

4. "It matters that the prevailing ethos of a company brings together corporate purpose and personal values". Cardinal Vincent Nichols

5. 'Serving the public and taking care of own's own employees are not an afterthought of business, but rather its very essence". Robert Solomon

6. 'It is hard to separate businesses being ethical for its own sake with the fact that being ethical might be good for business". Wilcockson and Wilkinson OCR Religious Studies (Hodder, 2016)

7. 'The solidarity that binds all men together as members of a common family make it impossible for wealthy nations to look with indifference upon the hunger, misery and poverty of other nations". Pope John XXIII.

8. "The natural environment is a collective good and the responsibility of everyone". Pope Francis

9. "Man should not consider his material possessions as his own, but as common to all, so as to share them without hesitation when others are in need." Thomas Aquinas (ST II-II, Q46, A2)

10. "The rights and duties of the employers, as compared with the rights and duties of the employed, ought to be the subject of careful consideration." Rerum Novarum 1891 (p 58)

The Four Questions Answered

In the first section of this book I mentioned that there are four questions we need to ask of any moral theory. They spell the acronym **DARM** (**D**erivation, **A**pplication, **R**ealism, **M**otivation).

1. How Is The Idea Of Goodness Derived?

Goodness has to come from somewhere – it is, after all a human construct. The normal candidates are three:

1. God or faith

2. Reason (a priori)

3. Observation or experience (a posteriori, from experience).

RELATIVISTS argue that our idea of goodness comes directly from **CULTURE** (what JL Mackie in Inventing Right and Wrong calls "forms of life") or from **EXPERIENCE** (the utilitarian or situationist view that we judge right and wrong according to circumstances and likely consequences).

NATURAL LAW theorists like **AQUINAS** argue that goodness is partly an **A PRIORI** idea given by God – what he calls synderesis "the intuitive knowledge of first principles", and partly an **A POSTERIORI** idea worked out by experience. We develop our conscience and practical wisdom by looking at circumstances . Natural Law goods are in the end

OBSERVABLE GOODS. We apply the **PRIMARY PRECEPTS** (acronym **POWER**) to situations.

KANT argues that morality is an **A PRIORI** category of the mind like number or cause and effect. Just as we need a concept of **NUMBER** before we can count, so we need a concept of the **CATEGORICAL IMPERATIVE** before we can apply it to the world and synthetic experience where we discover how it works. Morality is therefore **A PRIORI SYNTHETIC**.

UTLITARIANS see goodness as a **TELEOLOGICAL** idea depending on the end we pursue, either **PLEASURE** (the psychological "sovereign two masters, pleasure and pain" of Bentham) or **HAPPINESS** (it is good because most people desire it as an end in itself, says **MILL**). So goodness is measurable, an **OBJECTIVE, EMPIRICAL IDEA**, either by counting **HEDONS** (Bentham) or **DESIRES** (Mill). This is therefore a theory appealing to **A POSTERIORI** knowledge because we cannot know consequences without some experience of them.

Notice that only one theory is purely **DEONTOLOGICAL**, Kantian ethics. **NATURAL LAW** has deontological outcomes (the **SECONDARY PRECEPTS**) which come from a **TELEOLOGICAL WORLDVIEW** because in Natural law everything has a proper rational purpose (**TELOS**).

SITUATION ETHICS argues that goodness is accepted by faith as the supreme noram (**POSITIVISM**). Fletcher makes it clear that no intrinsic good can be proved (be it the good will, happiness or anything else). It has to be **POSITED**.

2. How Are The Theories Applied?

RELATIVISTS see goodness as relative to culture or experience and so any situation needs to be applied to the relevant cultural value. These may still be very **REASONABLE** but, argues the relativist, even **REASON** is culturally conditioned and not **PURE** as Kant implied.

NATURAL LAW THEORY applies the five primary precepts (acronym **POWER**) to produce the secondary precepts. So the **P** of **POWER** (preservation of life) yields the **SECONDARY PRECEPT** do not abort, do not commit suicide, do not murder. These are not **ABSOLUTE RULES** as we allow killing in time of war. Ultimately the primary precepts are derived from an idea of **HUMAN FLOURISHING** – what it means for a human being to live well or excellently.

KANT sees right and wrong as something irrational, a **CONTRADICTION** or logical inconsistency. There are two types of self contradiction: the **CONTRADICTION IN NATURE** includes suicide and breaking your promises. These cannot be willed universally without contradiction because **EUTHANASIA** if universalised leads to mass suicide of those in pain, and breaking your promise if universalised leads to the elimination of the idea of promising altogether. A **CONTRADICTION IN WILL** is not illogical, but cannot be universally willed or desired. We could never desire not to help our neighbour in distress because we would always want to be helped when we are in distress.

UTILITARIANS see the right action as one that maximises happiness or pleasure. So we need to examine the likely consequences, count how many are affected by our choice, and then apply the Greatest Happiness Principle. We apply utilitarian principles **CONSEQUENTIALLY**.

SITUATION ETHICS argues for a case by case, pragmatic approach that lies somewhere between **ANTINOMIANISM** (no rules) and **LEGALISM** (strict rules). This is a form of Christian relativism espoused by liberal Christians who see the primary command is to love unconditionally (not to judge or make legal demands). Here the person - their needs and desires - is the key. **PERSONALISM** requires we put them first. This can be described as a from of relativism, as Fletcher himself does - he calls it **PRINCIPLED RELATIVISM** because of the one principle or norm - **AGAPE** love, which is absolute and unchanging. But notice there are other definitions of relativism than Fletcher's - who sees goodness as relative to love and to the consequences and situation.

3. Realism

How realistic are these theories from the perspective of modern sciences such as **PSYCHOLOGY** and **BIOLOGY**?

RELATIVISM fits well the postmodern world where there is no one overarching narrative accepted as true. It also fits **FREUDIAN** psychology where conscience comes from our upbringing and the sense of shame engendered by our parents and teachers. In the postmodern age we are taught to tolerate difference.

NATURAL LAW is often condemned as outdated. However the idea of a shared rational nature is something evolutionary biologists accept. **RICHARD DAWKINS** (The Selfish Gene) talks of a "lust to be nice" coming from our evolved sense of obligation to one another. Is this so different from **AQUINAS'** synderesis rule that we by nature "do good and avoid evil"? Dawkins rejects the **TELEOLOGICAL** nature of Natural Law, as there is no purpose to **EVOLUTION**, he argues, just an endless struggle to survive. But we have inherited an **ALTRUISTIC GENE** from this battle of the genes giving us a shared moral nature. The selfish gene is the self-promoting gene, but for humans, it is in our interest to be moral and so, argues Dawkins, the selfish gene gives us our moral sense and desire to help others.

KANT's ethical theory can be criticised for being **DUALISTIC**. So he sees the world of experience, the **PHENOMENAL** world as opposed to the world of ideas, the **NOUMENAL** world. He also contrasts **REASON** and **EMOTION** in a way that seems to deny moral worth to an action done out of compassion rather than duty alone. The outcome of his theory, that categorical rules are **ABSOLUTE** can also be criticised as unrealistic. In practice we do lie to save someone's life – the goodness is situational, not absolute as Kant suggests.

SITUATION ETHICS suffers from the same two problems as utilitarianism. First, it requires an **IMPARTIALITY** which few are capable of, except Jesus himself. We all ten to rank pople accorsing tot heir closeness to us (family, friends, acquaintances, neighbours and finally strangers). But agape allows no such ranking, otherwise it becomes conditional love. Secondly, it is hard to predict **CONSEQUENCES** and this requires a lifetime of wisdom which few of us possess. William **BARCLAY** (Ethics in a Permissive Society) also points out that social rules embody such wisdom - and those that don't (such as 'homosexuality is wrong') become revised and rejected. But to focus just on individual need and choice is to ignore the important function of rules as guides for us. Ultimately, then Situation ethics may be too demanding and so unrealistic.

4. Motivation: Why Be Moral?

So we come to the final, and perhaps most pressing question. Why be moral at all? Why not live a life of selfish egoism and be a parasite on the goodness of everyone else?

RELATIVISM is a wide and amibiguous concept. Joseph Fletcher (Situation Ethics) defined himself as a relativist (Situation Ethics is a form of Christian relativism). He argued that we are moral out of love for fellow human beings. But this begs the question why I should bother about fellow human beings when it's not in my interest to do so? Fletcher's answer was that we need to convert to the way of love - commitment comes before action. He calls this **THEOLOGICAL POSITIVISM**. Situation ethics is something of a special case and is arguably not a pure form of relativism as it has one **ABSOLUTE** at its centre - agape love.

NATURAL LAW theorists argue from a **TELEOLOGICAL** standpoint. Be moral, they say, because it is reasonable to want to flourish as a human being – to be the most excellent person you can be. A knife should cut well, says Aristotle, and a human being should be rational in order to flourish well. **AQUINAS** argues that our greatest happiness will be found by aligning the natural law with God's eternal law. This will cause us to be a full, complete human being.

KANT takes the stern, dutiful line of obedience to the moral law or **CATEGORICAL IMPERATIVE**. He argues that rational people will freely choose this way as the most logically consistent way of arriving at the **SUMMUM BONUM**, the greatest good. Autonomous human beings will realise that to obey the categorical imperative out of duty is the best way of building the best of all conceivable moral worlds. Like Kant himself, this moral law within should fill us with awe. It's wonderful. The summum bonum is a mixture of virtue (dutifulness) and happiness ultimately only discovered in heaven (Kant's postulate of **IMMORTALITY**).

UTILITARIANS are not agreed on what motivates us. **BENTHAM** thought we were psychological **HEDONISTS** motivated by the prospect of pleasure and avoiding pain. **MILL** disagreed. He thought pleasure and happiness were not the same, as happiness needed clear goals and strenuous activities. Happiness is to be found in challenges met and difficulties overcome – which sometimes can involve discipline and sacrifice. Why bother with the happiness of others? Mill answered, out of **SYMPATHY** for my fellow human beings. "In the Golden Rule of Jesus of Nazareth ("do to others as you would have them do to you" Matthew 7:18)", wrote Mill, "is all the ethics of utility".

SITUATION ETHICS requires us to commit to the motive of unconditional love - we accept this by faith (**POSITIVISM**). Fletcher doesn't talk much about motive, but the Bible suggests 'we love because God first loved us' (1 John 4:19). So we are motivated by what God in Jesus Christ has first done for us in sacrificing his life for us and suffering pain and humiliation on the cross. Moreover Christ's death liberated us from the slavery to sin and set a new agenda for us - to establish the kingdom of God. This is a kingdom of love. And God gave us the Holy Spirit - the spirit of love in our hearts - to empower us when we find it impossible.

Free Sample Chapter

From

How To Write Philosophical Essays

The Night Before the Exam

I have assumed throughout his book that you are an exam candidate, and so I want to write a chapter for you to read the night before the exam, which distills the advice we have been trying to demonstrate here.

Essentially there are two methods of writing essays on Philosophy, Ethics and Christian Thought.

METHOD 1: The thesis approach **TIDE**

In this approach, discussed in the second chapter, we state our thesis (conclusion) early in the first paragraph. We then develop the thesis in the body of the essay, illustrating it briefly and intelligently and presenting contrasting views if we so wish, (which we reject with good reasons). The thesis is then restated in a slightly fuller way (to reflect the careful analysis that precedes it) as a conclusion. **We should use this method when we are confident we understand the question and its implications**.

METHOD 2: The 'ask questions about the question' approach **AQUAQ**

Quite often we may not be very confident about what the question is driving at. If this is the case, then we must adopt the tactic of interrogating the question or asking questions about the question. I suggest we ask three questions and then spend a paragraph answering each one before coming to a conclusion. Each question focuses on one element of the exam question. **We should use this method when we are not fully confident about what the question involves.**

An example might help here. Suppose I have a question on ethics which asks:

"The ethical issues around abortion cannot be resolved without first resolving the issue of personhood".

What are the ethical issues surrounding abortion? How and with what ethical tools are these issues resolved? What is meant by the concept of personhood? These three questions (none of which have a single answer), woven into an opening paragraph, give the answer a clear, relevant structure - and the thesis should emerge as we develop our essay. The conclusion is then presented as our own answer to these three questions, perhaps arrived at by contrasting the views of specific philosophers and setting up two ethical theories to see how the idea of personhood is relevant to each.

An equivalent example in Philosophy might address the title "Religious Language is meaningless.", Discuss. The questions you might ask in your opening paragraph might include: What do we mean by religious language? Are there different rules for religious language when compared to everyday language? How is the word 'meaning' to be understood?

When you arrive in the exam room, you must follow the steps set out below.

Read every question and highlight key words

Every year candidates make the fundamental error of learning a previous essay off by heart and then regurgitating it in the exam. And every year the examiner complains that candidates did not answer the question. So take a highlighter pen in with you and

1. Highlight all the **trigger/command** words (words like "explain", "to what extent", "discuss"). And then

2. Highlight any words that are **unusual** or unexpected.

If the trigger word is **explain** it is not asking us to **evaluate**. For example "explain the main principles of classical utilitarianism" has the unusual word "classical" in there. By focusing on this word and highlighting it, you are forced to ask the question "what is classical utilitarianism?" and so there is at least a chance that you will avoid the irrelevance of talking about Peter Singer, who is a modern utilitarian.

For Philosophy, sometimes a very specific question is asked to highlight an aspect of an argument, for example, 'Explain Descartes' ontological argument for the existence of God'. It won't gain marks if you go through other ontological arguments as this is not what the question is asking (you could highlight one or two differences, but only to stress the points that Descartes is making). Remember that when a scholar is mentioned in the syllabus, the question can be entirely addressed to that scholar - so the night before go through the syllabus check which scholars might come up.

But (just to be absolutely clear about this) at **A2 level** we are expected to interweave analysis and evaluation, and this is made clear by trigger words such as "discuss", "assess" or "to what extent".

Sketch out your thesis/ key questions about the question

Always make sure there is some additional loose paper on your desk (put your hand up before the exam starts and request it). Then sketch out quickly your thesis, the main points you need to develop it, and any illustrations you may use. If you are genuinely unsure about the question, don't worry: every other candidate is probably unsure as well. Then use method 2 and ask three questions about the question and impose your own interpretation on it. You will gain credit by this considered and well-directed line which will then emerge as your answer.

My strong advice would be to practise sequencing ideas before the exam, and to have you own mind-map prepared and memorised which you can quickly sketch on a piece of paper as a memory aid.

Be bold in your answer

It's surprising how many candidates come up with statements such as "there are many arguments for and against the ontological argument, and the issue remains difficult to resolve". This is a form of intellectual cowardice which gains no marks at all. Be bold in what you argue, and try hard to justify your approach with good, solid reasons. It is the quality of the argument which gains credit in philosophical writing, not the conclusion you arrive at. Of course, it essential that the conclusion follows.

Analyse, don't just assert

It is tempting to throw down everything you know about, say, utilitarianism in a series of unconnected assertions.

"Utilitarianism is teleological, consequentialist and relativistic. It sets up the Greatest Happiness Principle. Utilitarians also believe the end justifies the means."

These are just assertions which are peppered liberally with what we call technical language (that is language no-one in the real world ever uses). Notice that the above opening few lines demonstrate no understanding and no analytical ability. Instead we should be aiming to write more like this:

"Utilitarianism is a theory of rational desire which holds to one intrinsic good: pleasure or happiness. By the greatest happiness principle utilitarians seek to maximise this good in two ways: they seek to maximise net happiness (happiness minus misery) for the maximum number of people. So it is an aggregating theory, where goodness is added up from individual desires to produce an overall maximum good in which "everyone counts as one" (Bentham)."

You should avoid phrases like 'this famous philosopher' and 'this issue has been debated for centuries'. Is this true? How would we know? Avoid these kinds of broad, sweeping generalisations.

Illustrate your argument

I remember reading an exam report at University which mentioned that one candidate had been highly commended in an essay on utilitarianism for discussing the case of Captain Oates who, during Scott's doomed Antarctic expedition in 1912, walked out of the storm-bound tent in order to sacrifice himself to save his friends, with the words "I may be gone some considerable time". It's an interesting example because it suggests that a utilitarian could be capable of heroic sacrifice rather than the usual illustration candidates give of torturing a terror suspect to find a bomb location.

Spend a few moments working out which examples you will discuss to illustrate key theories and their application. You can pre-prepare them especially in Ethics, and in Philosophy of Religion you can pre-prepare the contrasting arguments which philosophers bring to many of the syllabus areas.

In Philosophy of Religion this advice applies especially to areas such as religious language and the analogies told by Flew (Wisdom's gardener), Hare (three blik illustrations) and Mitchell, (The Stranger), though be concise in how you illustrate these examples - always make them serve the point you are making and not the other way round.

What is the examiner looking for?

In summary the examiner is looking for three things:

Relevance - every sentence linked to the question set and to your main thesis.

Coherence - every sentence and paragraph should "hang together' or cohere. The linkages should be clear as the analysis proceeds.

Clarity - your style should be clear, and in the context, the philosophical vocabulary you use should be clear. You don't necessarily have to define every technical word, but if it does need a little clarification, you can always use brackets for economy. For example:

"Utilitarianism is a teleological (end-focused) theory combining an idea of intrinsic goodness with a method of assessing that goodness by considering consequences".

An example in philosophy would be:

"The Falsification Principle argues that for any statement to be treated as a proposition it must deny at least one state of affairs rather than affirm all outcomes by expanding its criteria, (and in doing so, 'dying the death of a thousand qualifications', as Flew notes)."

Postscript

Peter Baron read Politics, Philosophy and Economics at New College, Oxford and afterwards obtained an MLitt for a research degree in Hermeneutics at Newcastle University. He qualified as an Economics teacher in 1982, and taught ethics at Wells Cathedral School in Somerset from 2006-2012. He is currently a freelance writer and speaker.

In 2007 he set up a philosophy and ethics community dedicated to enlarging the teaching of philosophy in schools by applying the theory of multiple intelligences to the analysis of philosophical and ethical problems. So far over 700 schools have joined the community and over 30,000 individuals use his website every month.

To join the community please join our mailing list on peped.org or follow Peped on Facebook. We welcome contributions and suggestions so that our community continues to flourish and expand.

www.peped.org

Printed in Great Britain
by Amazon